BILL OF RIGHTS

THE ORIGIN OF BRITAIN'S DEMOCRACY

BILL
OF
RIGHTS

BODLEIAN
LIBRARY
PUBLISHING

INTRODUCTION

The Bill of Rights 1689 is the foundation of the British parliamentary state. It followed the deposition of King James II, marking the victory of Parliament in its long struggle with the Stuart kings. In one sense it was a backward-looking document, a response to the delinquencies of the Stuart kings, some of which are of purely historical interest today. In another it led to the development of the principles which lie at the heart of Britain's unwritten constitution to this day: that Parliament is the supreme organ of the state, and that the monarch's ministers govern in the name of the Crown but are answerable to Parliament for all that they do. The Bill of Rights did not introduce democracy to

Britain. That happened long afterwards with the gradual expansion of the parliamentary franchise. But it provided the constitutional framework in which democracy was possible without a revolution. It was a large part of the reason for the remarkable political stability of Britain over the next three and a half centuries.

Seventeenth-century Englishmen believed in monarchy but also in a number of principles which can fairly be called republican. They believed in the dispersal of power. They believed in government by consent, expressed in a representative Parliament which alone could authorize the levying of taxes or a change in the law. They believed in the common law, which had begun to emerge at the beginning of the century as a conservative force, constraining the expansion of royal power. Religion was a critical part of the political identity of the English. The Church of England was established by law. The law upheld as privileged its doctrine and its rituals. But Protestantism was as much a political position as a religious one. The great majority of Englishmen associated Catholicism with an autocratic model of government exemplified by the absolute monarchy of Louis XIV of France, which they firmly rejected. 'No popery, No slavery' was the motto which the London MPs embroidered on their hat ribbons in Charles II's last Parliament.

The four Stuart kings who reigned between 1603 and 1688 were closer to the spirit of their age than their subjects. They believed that government was a charge from God, to whom they were answerable for its exercise. They believed that they were entitled to take whatever steps were necessary to discharge their responsibility for the government of the realm. These were constitutional orthodoxies in continental monarchies. The kings of France levied taxes, changed the law and enforced compliance, all by royal ordinance. The basic problem of the Stuart kings was that they were charged with the administration and defence of the state but lacked the means to do it. There was no national administration to carry the king's authority into the furthest reaches of the land. At a local level the greater landowners and municipal corporations served as an intermediate layer of government, and yet neither of them were subject to the commands of the king or his ministers. The Crown had only a small standing army at its disposal (8,000 men in 1680), which would not have been enough to suppress a major rebellion. Apart from some traditional taxes on trade, the king had no tax-raising powers of his own. In the absence of any consensus about the distribution of power within the state, the differences between the Stuarts and the great majority of their subjects were bound to emerge as a source of political instability.

The main battleground was taxation. The English Parliament was summoned, prorogued or dissolved at the king's discretion, and sat for only a few weeks. It was therefore incapable of exercising a general supervision of government. But it was the only body which could authorize the imposition and collection of taxes. All four Stuart kings had to deal with recalcitrant Parliaments which sought to impose changes of policy in areas that the kings regarded as their own, such as religion, foreign policy and the armed forces. In March 1629 Charles I dissolved Parliament, declaring his intention of ruling without them owing to the 'malevolent dispositions of some ill-affected persons of the House of Commons'. For a decade his government was funded by a variety of taxes and forced loans imposed without parliamentary authority in the face of mounting resistance. When in 1639 a major rebellion broke out in Scotland he was forced to summon Parliament again and found himself at its mercy. The outcome was a civil war, the execution of the king and a short-lived republic which never overcame the stain of illegitimacy.

The tensions which had provoked the civil war did not disappear with the restoration of the monarchy in 1660. Neither Charles II (1660–1685) nor his brother James II (1685–1688) was trusted.

Charles was a crypto-Catholic, and James a declared one. Both were allies and pensioners of the king of France for most of their reigns. There were issues between them and their Parliaments about the legal status of Catholics, the conduct of foreign policy, the maintenance of armed forces, the perceived wastage of the king's revenues, the competence of his ministers and the succession to the throne. In January 1681 Charles II dissolved Parliament, declaring in terms reminiscent of his father that he must rule without it owing to 'the restless malice of ill men who are labouring to poison our people'. James II prorogued his only Parliament indefinitely after it refused to enact legislation to relieve Catholics of the disabilities imposed on them by statute. The result of this stand-off was that no parliamentary taxes were voted for a decade after 1679. The government subsisted in those years on French subsidies.

Opposition to James II was motivated mainly by fear that his accession presaged the erection of an absolute monarchy. These fears seemed to be borne out by James's acts. Having failed to get Parliament to lift the disabilities inflicted on Catholics, he sought to do so under the royal prerogative, by declaring that they would no longer be enforced. He used the prerogative to suppress or disable alternative sources of power, for example by revoking municipal and colonial charters, giving directions to bishops and universities, marginalizing judges thought to be unsympathetic and trying to pack Parliament with his supporters.

In the last years of Charles II there had been a sustained campaign in Parliament to exclude Catholics in general and James II in particular from the succession to the throne. The object was to divert the succession to James's daughters Mary and Anne, both of whom were staunch Protestants. Mary, the older daughter, was married to William of Orange, the *stadtholder* of the Dutch Republic. In the summer of 1688 a group of prominent noblemen wrote inviting William to invade. It was never clear whether their object was to depose the king, but events soon resolved the ambiguity. William landed at Torbay on 5 November 1688 with an army of 15,000 men. James's fleet and army melted away, and he himself fled to France.

The Bill of Rights was the first of a number of statutes enacted by a 'Convention' which met on 22 January 1689 to fill the constitutional void left by the disappearance of James II. The Convention was not technically a Parliament. It had been summoned by William of Orange at a time when he was not yet king, on the authority of a group of privy councillors and members of the last Parliament of Charles II, who happened to be in London. But the Convention was very like a Parliament. It was constituted by election of the Commons and personal summonses of the Lords in exactly the same way as a Parliament, and in due course declared itself to be one. The smell of technical irregularity always hung around the acts of the Convention, and to put the matter beyond doubt they were duly ratified by the next Parliament in 1690.

On 13 February 1689 the Convention issued a 'Declaration of Right', declaring that James II 'did endeavour to subvert and extirpate the Protestant religion and the laws and liberties of this kingdom'. It asserted that since his flight to France the throne had been vacant. It then listed his various abuses, which were declared to be 'utterly and directly contrary to the known laws and statutes and freedom of this realm'. The Declaration resolved to offer the throne to William of Orange and Mary, implicitly on the basis that they accepted its terms. On 23 February 1689 they accepted both the offer and the Declaration. The Convention subsequently enacted the Declaration of Right as a statute, which received royal assent on 16 December 1689.

The original title of the Bill of Rights was 'An Act declaring the Rights and Liberties of the Subject and Settling the Succession of the Crown.' It shortly became known as the Bill of Rights, a title that was formally given to it by the Short Titles Act of 1896. It was not, however, a bill of rights in the sense in which that phrase is used today. It was not concerned with recognizing the rights of the individual against the state. Even the rights which at first sight look like individual rights, such as the prohibition of excessive bail or fines and 'cruel punishments' in criminal proceedings or the right of Protestants (only) to bear arms for their defence, were in reality designed to enable citizens collectively to resist the overreaching acts of the state. What the authors of the Bill of Rights meant by the 'rights and liberties' of the subject was their right to have their grievances redressed by a free and representative Parliament and to live under the common law with only such changes as Parliament approved. Because Parliament was regarded as synonymous with freedom, the object of the Bill of Rights was to protect and in some respects enhance its constitutional role.

The Bill of Rights required Parliaments to be held 'frequently'. This was later defined by the Triennial Act 1694 as meaning that a new Parliament must be summoned at least every three years (subsequently increased to seven). In practice it had to meet more frequently than that, because the Bill of Rights restated the long-standing principle that money could not be levied for the use of the Crown without parliamentary authority. It also required parliamentary approval for the maintenance of a standing army in peacetime. The practice was to pass annual Mutiny Acts, valid for a year at a time, which provided the sole legal basis on which soldiers could be required to obey orders. Other provisions reinforced the authority and independence of Parliament, by forbidding the king to suspend any laws 'by regal authority' or to interfere with free elections. The famous ninth clause provided that 'the freedom of Speech and debates or proceedings in Parliament ought not to be impeached in any court or place out of Parliament.'

William III's relations with Parliament were not always harmonious. He vetoed more legislation than any of his Stuart predecessors. He resisted parliamentary criticism of his foreign policy, as they had. He gave his consent to the Triennial Act through gritted teeth. He complained of the 'mass of impertinences' which Parliament inflicted on him in terms that sounded very like Charles I and Charles II. But his main preoccupation was the great succession of wars against Louis XIV of France. His dependence on English revenues and manpower for his wars forced him to concede Parliament's claims to primacy in the state. In the decade before the accession of William and Mary, there had been five parliamentary sessions and the Commons conducted business on a total of 171 days. In the decade afterwards there were eleven sessions and the Commons conducted business on nearly 1,300 days. On average in the early eighteenth century the Commons sat for between a third and a half of each year. In the two decades after the Glorious Revolution, there were ten general elections.

It fell to the political philosopher John Locke to provide a rationale for these changes. Locke wrote his *Essay of Civil Government* in 1689 to justify the Glorious Revolution to the world. He argued for a principle of conservative revolution. The king derived his powers not from God but from an implicit contract with his subjects.

His powers were conferred on him in trust for the benefit of society as a whole. He might forfeit them if he broke his trust. In that case, society continued, and might take whatever steps were needed to ensure continuity of government and the preservation of life and property.

The events of 1688–89 came to be called the 'Glorious Revolution', but the authors of the Bill of Rights did not regard themselves as revolutionaries. They believed themselves to be restoring the ancient principles of the constitution. They professed to be declaring the law as it had stood before its violation by James II. The House of Lords would not even accept that James had been deposed. They rejected the Commons' original draft of the Declaration of Rights, which had asserted that he had forfeited the Crown by his breach of faith with his subjects, and insisted instead on the fiction that he had abdicated.

In spite of the professed conservatism of its authors, the Bill of Rights had important consequences for the whole subsequent development of the British state, and remains to this day the source of some of its most fundamental constitutional principles. It led, over the following half-century, to a transformation of the relationship between the Crown and its ministers. Seventeenth-century kings had a legally and practically unfettered right to choose their own ministers regardless of parliamentary sentiment. The only way in which Parliament could get rid of ministers who enjoyed the confidence of the monarch was by impeachment. This was a criminal procedure initiated by the elected House and tried by the Lords. It was wholly inappropriate for dealing with a minister who was simply unpopular, incompetent or wedded to policies of which the Commons disapproved. It became obsolete because the growing dependence of the government on parliamentary support made it unnecessary. The support could simply be withdrawn. The government would then be without authority to raise taxes or maintain an army. The last impeachment of ministers on purely political grounds was in 1713. The ministers of Queen Anne were impeached for their part in negotiating the Treaty of Utrecht, which brought an end to the Continental wars of the two previous decades. In 1742 Sir Robert Walpole was the first prime minister to resign solely because he had lost the confidence of the Commons.

By then it was well established that the ministry was nominated by the monarch but answerable to the elected chamber of

Parliament for everything that they did on the king's behalf. This included acts done in the exercise of the royal prerogative, such as the conduct of foreign policy and military operations. The king's government must have the confidence of the House of Commons and must resign if they lost it. Parliament became the supreme legislative and political organ of the state and the sole ultimate source of a government's political legitimacy.

Britain is commonly said to have no written constitution, although much of it is written, in statutes such as the Bill of Rights. There is, however, a more important sense in which Britain does not have a written constitution. There is no body of constitutional law which prevails over all other sources of law. There is nothing which counts, in the words of the United States

Constitution, as the 'supreme law of the land' to which all other laws and practices of the state must conform. Even the Bill of Rights could in theory be repealed by a simple majority in both houses of Parliament.

In the absence of a code of fundamental law, the only supreme principle of the British Constitution is the sovereignty of Parliament. It may enact or repeal any law whatsoever. The only limit on its competence is conceptual rather than legal. No Parliament can bind its successors, for a future Parliament will always be free to use its plenitude of power to untie the bond.

The unconfined sovereignty of Parliament was not a rule of law. No statute proclaimed it in terms. No judicial decision announced it. It was the result of the way in which the authors of the Glorious Revolution chose to confine the exercise of monarchical power.

They did not sweep the royal prerogative away. They did not even limit it. The royal prerogative remained intact but its exercise was brought under parliamentary control. This was not just because taxation and military service were expressly subject to parliamentary consent. It was because in due course the remaining prerogative powers came to be exercised on the Crown's behalf by ministers responsible to Parliament. In effect the sovereignty of the Crown passed to Parliament. But whereas in the king's hands it was constrained by law, Parliament could fashion the law as it saw fit.

The British constitutional model is almost unique. Almost every other country in the world has rejected the concept of unlimited legislative sovereignty. The United States led the way, with a constitution which was not only the first but the most influential. The US Constitution is a code of fundamental law. It lays down limits to what even Congress can do. The president is directly elected and derives a large part of his authority directly from the Constitution, and not only from congressional legislation and congressional support. Congress may have no confidence in the president, but it cannot get rid of him short of impeachment for high crimes or misdemeanours.

Almost every country in the world has chosen to follow the American model. No doubt Britain would have done so too if some cataclysmic event had made it necessary to rebuild the state from the foundations up. Disaster is the godfather of almost every written constitution. The occasions for adopting written constitutions with written codes of fundamental law are revolution, foreign invasion, secession, decolonization and any other event which destroys the existing structure of the state. Britain did not experience this in the Glorious Revolution and certainly has not experienced it since.

The British model was not challenged until quite recently. There was an almost complete consensus in the eighteenth and nineteenth centuries that Britain was a paradigm of constitutional excellence. The constitutional settlement of 1689 was viewed with uncritical reverence by Englishmen from the cautious reflections of Edmund Burke to the complacent prejudices of Dickens's Mr Podsnap. Their veneration was shared by many foreign commentators, including those who came from countries which had adopted a very different constitutional model. American historians traced the values of their public life back to principles imported from England.

French political scientists like Alexis de Tocqueville and historians like Elie Halévie looked to England as a haven of enlightened constitutional stability.

It was only in the second half of the twentieth century that confidence in the British model began to wane. The past century has been an age of intensive government. The executive enjoys vast discretionary powers, far wider and potentially more intrusive than the prerogatives asserted by James II. Most of them have been conferred by statute, but in terms so general as to leave all the relevant judgements to ministers. At the same time, the power of the executive over the House of Commons has been enhanced by tighter party discipline, a larger payroll vote, and the emergence of a more presidential style of government as voters increasingly decided between candidates at general elections according to the perceived qualities of their party leader.

People began to question the basic assumption of the revolutionaries of 1689 that the rights of the citizen were sufficiently protected by a combination of the common law and parliamentary oversight. The consensus that once supported the parliamentary state broke down. A division emerged between those who argued for a source of fundamental law superior to Parliament, with a higher degree of judicial oversight, and those who contended that only an elected legislature had the democratic legitimacy to perform these functions. One suggested answer to this last group has been a greater reliance on non-parliamentary sources of consent, such as referenda or citizens' assemblies.

The tension between these approaches has given a renewed relevance to the Bill of

Rights and its legacy. There has been more judicial consideration of the Bill of Rights in the last sixty years than in the whole of the previous 270. There have been decisions about charges for government services without express parliamentary authority, which has been equated with unauthorised taxation (*Attorney-General* v. *Wilts United Dairies* (1922) 38 TLR 781 (CA); *Congreve* v. *Home Office* [1976] QB 629 (CA); about the power to suspend Parliamentary legislation (*Gouriet* v. *Union of Post Office Workers* [1977] QB 729 and [1978] AC 435 (HL); *Pretty* v. *Director of Public Prosecutions* [2002] 1 AC 800 (HL); and about the immunity of Parliamentary proceedings from review in the courts (*Associated Newspapers Ltd* v. *Dingle* [1960] 2 QB 405 and [1964] AC 371 (HL); *Prebble* v. *Television of New Zealand Ltd* [1995] 1 AC 321). The Bill of Rights has even taken on some of the characteristics of a supreme law. In *R (HS2 Action Alliance Limited)* v. *Secretary of State for Transport* [2014] 1 WLR 324 (SC), the Supreme Court suggested that even the overriding provisions of European law (which then applied to the UK) could not authorize it to question the quality of the legislative process in Parliament.

Since 2019 the courts of both England and Scotland have had to deal with major litigation about the fundamentals of the constitution. Some of this litigation has arisen from challenges to parliamentary legislation or to policies sanctioned by Parliament. Some of it has arisen from challenges to parliamentary oversight by the government itself. Recent decisions of the Supreme Court have restored, at any rate at the legal level, the traditional principle of the centrality of Parliament and the legacy of the Bill of Rights. In *R (Miller)* v. *Secretary of State for Exiting the European Union* [2018] AC 61 and *R (Miller)* v. *The Prime Minister* [2020] AC 373, the Supreme Court rejected two attempts by the executive at a time when no party commanded a majority in the House of Commons, to restrict parliamentary control over Britain's departure from the European Union. These cases have led to the rediscovery of Parliament as the source of political legitimacy. In the first of them, the Court quoted with approval the observation of the great Victorian constitutional scholar A.V. Dicey that 'the judges know nothing about the will of the people except in so far as that will is expressed by an Act of Parliament.' In the second, they reaffirmed the centrality of Parliament in a declaration that perfectly encapsulated the reasoning behind the Bill of Rights. It is through Parliament, they held, that 'the policies of the executive are subjected to consideration by the representatives of the electorate, the executive is required to report, explain and defend its actions, and citizens are protected from the arbitrary exercise of executive power.' The authorities cited for this proposition were the series of statutes between 1688 and 1707 which followed the Glorious Revolution. Foremost among them was the Bill of Rights 1689.

Jonathan Sumption

Bill of Rights, London 1689

An Act declareing the Rights and Liberties of the Subject and Setleing the Succession of the Crowne.

WHEREAS the Lords Spirituall and Temporall and Com[m]ons assembled at Westminster lawfully fully and freely representing all the Estates of the People of this Realme did upon the thirteenth day of February in the yeare of our Lord one thousand six hundred eighty eight present unto their Majesties then called and known by the Names and Stile of William and Mary Prince and Princesse of Orange being present in their proper Persons a certaine Declaration in Writeing made by the said Lords and Com[m]ons in the Words following viz

Whereas the late King James the Second by the Assistance of diverse evill Councellors Judges and Ministers imployed by him did endeavour to subvert and extirpate the Protestant Religion and the Lawes and Liberties of this Kingdome.

Dispensing and Suspending Power.

By Assumeing and Exerciseing a Power of Dispensing with and Suspending of Lawes and the Execution of Lawes without Consent of Parlyament.

Committing Prelates.

By Committing and Prosecuting diverse Worthy Prelates for humbly Petitioning to be excused from Concurring to the said Assumed Power.

Ecclesiastical Commission.

By issueing and causeing to be executed a Commission under the Great Seale for Erecting a Court called The Court of Commissioners for Ecclesiasticall Causes.

Levying Money.

By Levying Money for and to the Use of the Crowne by p[re]tence of Prerogative for other time and in other manner then the same was granted by Parlyament.

Standing Army.

By raising and keeping a Standing Army within this Kingdome in time of Peace without Consent of Parlyament and Quartering Soldiers contrary to Law.

Disarming Protestants, &c.

By causing severall good Subjects being

Protestants to be disarmed at the same time when Papists were both Armed and Imployed contrary to Law.

Violating Elections.

By Violating the Freedome of Election of Members to serve in Parlyament.

Illegal Prosecutions.

By Prosecutions in the Court of Kings Bench for Matters and Causes congizable onely in Parlyament and by diverse other Arbitrary and Illegall Courses.

Juries.

And whereas of late yeares Partiall Corrupt and Unqualifyed Persons have beene returned and served on Juryes in Tryalls and particularly diverse Jurors in Tryalls for High Treason which were not Freeholders,

Excessive Bail.

And excessive Baile hath beene required of Persons committed in Criminall Cases to elude the Benefitt of the Lawes made for the Liberty of the Subjects.

Fines.

And excessive Fines have beene imposed.

Punishments.

And illegall and cruell Punishments inflicted.

Grants of Fines, &c. before Conviction, &c.

And severall Grants and Promises made of Fines and Forfeitures before any Conviction or Judgement against the Persons upon whome the same were to be levyed.

All which are utterly and directly contrary to the knowne Lawes and Statutes and Freedome of this Realme.

*Recital that the late King James II.
had abdicated the Government, and that the
Throne was vacant, and that the Prince of
Orange had written Letters to the Lords and
Commons for the choosing Representatives
in Parliament.*

And whereas the said late King James the
Second haveing Abdicated the Government
and the Throne being thereby Vacant His
Hignesse the Prince of Orange (whome
it hath pleased Almighty God to make
the glorious Instrument of Delivering this
Kingdome from Popery and Arbitrary
Power) did (by the Advice of the Lords
Spirituall and Temporall and diverse
principall Persons of the Commons)
cause Letters to be written to the Lords
Spirituall and Temporall being Protestants
and other Letters to the severall Countyes
Cityes Universities Burroughs and Cinque
Ports for the Choosing of such Persons

to represent them as were of right to be sent to Parlyament to meete and sitt at Westminster upon the two and twentyeth day of January in this Yeare one thousand six hundred eighty and eight in order to such an Establishment as that their Religion Lawes and Liberties might not againe be in danger of being Subverted, Upon which Letters Elections haveing beene accordingly made.

The Subject's Rights.

And thereupon the said Lords Spirituall and Temporall and Commons pursuant to their respective Letters and Elections being now assembled in a full and free Representative of this Nation takeing into their most serious Consideration the best meanes for attaining the Ends aforesaid Doe in the first place (as their Auncestors in like Case have usually done) for the Vindicating and Asserting their auntient Rights and Liberties, Declare

Dispensing Power.

That the pretended Power of Suspending of Laws or the Execution of Laws by Regall Authority without Consent of Parlyament is illegall.

Late dispensing Power.

That the pretended Power of Suspending of Laws or the Execution of Laws by Regall Authority as it hath beene assumed and exercised of late is illegall.

Ecclesiastical Courts illegal.

That the Commission for erecting the late Court of Commissioners for Ecclesiasticall Causes and all other Commissions and Courts of like nature are Illegall and Pernicious.

Levying Money.

That levying Money for or to the Use of the

Crowne by p[re]tence of Prerogative without Grant of Parlyament for longer time or in other manner then the same is or shall be granted is Illegall.

Right to petition.

That it is the Right of the Subjects to petition the King and all Commitments and Prosecutions for such Petitioning are Illegall.

Standing Army.

That the raising or keeping a standing Army within the Kingdome in time of Peace unlesse it be with Consent of Parlyament is against Law.

Subjects' Arms.

That the Subjects which are Protestants may have Arms for their Defence suitable to their Conditions and as allowed by Law.

Freedom of Election.

That Election of Members of Parlyament ought to be free.

Freedom of Speech.

That the Freedome of Speech and Debates or Proceedings in Parlyament ought not to be impeached or questioned in any Court or Place out of Parlyament.

Excessive Bail.

That excessive Baile ought not to be required nor excessive Fines imposed nor cruell and unusuall Punishments inflicted.

Juries.

That Jurors ought to be duely impannelled and returned and Jurors which passe upon Men in Trialls for High Treason ought to be Freeholders.

Grants of Forfeitures.

That all Grants and Promises of Fines and Forfeitures of particular persons before Conviction are illegall and void.

Frequent Parliaments.

And that for Redresse of all Grievances and for the amending strengthening and preserveing of the Lawes Parlyaments ought to be held frequently.

The said Rights claimed; Tender of the Crown; Regal Power exercised; Limitation of the Crown; New Oaths of Allegiance, &c.

And they doe Claime Demand and Insist upon all and singular the Premises as their undoubted Rights and Liberties and that noe Declarations Judgements Doeings or Proceedings to the Prejudice of the People in any of the said Premisses ought in any wise to be drawne hereafter into Consequence or Example. To which Demand of their Rights they are particularly encouraged by the Declaration of his Highnesse the Prince of Orange as being the onely meanes for obtaining a full Redresse and Remedy therein. Haveing therefore an intire Confidence That his said Highnesse the Prince of Orange will perfect the Deliverance soe farr advanced by him and will still preserve them from the Violation of their Rights which they have here asserted and from all other Attempts upon their Religion Rights and Liberties. The said Lords Spirituall and Temporall and Commons assembled at Westminster doe Resolve That William and Mary Prince and Princesse of Orange be and be declared King and Queene of England France and Ireland and the Dominions thereunto belonging to hold the Crowne and Royall Dignity of the said Kingdomes and Dominions to them the said Prince and Princesse dureing their Lives and the Life of the Survivour of them And that the sole and full Exercise of the Regall Power be onely in and executed by the said Prince of Orange in the Names of the said Prince and Princesse dureing their joynt Lives And after their Deceases the said Crowne and Royall Dignitie of the said Kingdoms and Dominions to be to the Heires of the Body of the said Princesse And for default of such Issue to the Princesse Anne of Denmarke and the Heires of her Body And for default of such Issue to the Heires of the Body of the said Prince of Orange. And the Lords Spirituall and Temporall and Commons doe pray the said Prince and Princesse to accept the same accordingly. And that the Oathes hereafter mentioned be taken by all Persons of whome the Oathes of Allegiance and Supremacy might be required by Law instead of them And that the said Oathes of Allegiance and Supremacy be abrogated.

Allegiance.

I A B doe sincerely promise and sweare That I will be faithfull and beare true Allegiance to their Majestyes King William and Queene Mary Soe helpe me God.

Supremacy.

I A B doe sweare That I doe from my Heart Abhorr, Detest and Abjure as Impious and Hereticall this damnable Doctrine and Position That Princes Excommunicated or Deprived by the Pope or any Authority of the See of Rome may be deposed or murdered by their Subjects or any other whatsoever. And I doe declare That noe Forreigne Prince Person Prelate, State or Potentate hath or ought to have any Jurisdiction Power Superiority Preeminence or Authoritie Ecclesiasticall or Spirituall within this Realme Soe helpe me God.

Acceptance of the Crown; The Two Houses to sit; Subjects Liberties to be allowed, and Ministers hereafter to serve according to the same; William and Mary declared King and Queen. Limitation of the Crown; Papists debarred the Crown; Every King, &c. shall make the Declaration of 30 Car. II; If under 12 Years old, to be done after Attainment thereof; King's and Queen's Assent.

Upon which their said Majestyes did accept the Crowne and Royall Dignitie of the Kingdoms of England France and Ireland

and the Dominions thereunto belonging according to the Resolution and Desire of the said Lords and Commons contained in the said Declaration. And thereupon their Majestyes were pleased That the said Lords Spirituall and Temporall and Commons being the two Houses of Parlyament should continue to sitt and with their Majesties Royall Concurrence make effectuall Provision for the Setlement of the Religion Lawes and Liberties of this Kingdome soe that the same for the future might not be in danger againe of being subverted, To which the said Lords Spirituall and Temporall and Commons did agree and proceede to act accordingly. Now in pursuance of the Premisses the said Lords Spirituall and Temporall and Commons in Parlyament assembled for the ratifying confirming and establishing the said Declaration and the

Articles Clauses Matters and Things therein contained by the Force of a Law made in due Forme by Authority of Parlyament doe pray that it may be declared and enacted That all and singular the Rights and Liberties asserted and claimed in the said Declaration are the true auntient and indubitable Rights and Liberties of the People of this Kingdome and soe shall be esteemed allowed adjudged deemed and taken to be and that all and every the particulars aforesaid shall be firmly and strictly holden and observed as they are expressed in the said Declaration And all Officers and Ministers whatsoever shall serve their Majestyes and their Successors according to the same in all times to come. And the said Lords Spirituall and Temporall and Commons seriously considering how it hath pleased Almighty God in his marvellous Providence and mercifull Goodness to

this Nation to provide and preserve their
said Majestyes Royall Persons most happily
to Raigne over us upon the Throne of their
Auncestors for which they render unto him
from the bottome of their Hearts their
humblest Thanks and Praises doe truely
firmely assuredly and in the Sincerity of their
Hearts thinke and doe hereby recognize
acknowledge and declare That King James the
Second haveing abdicated the Government
and their Majestyes haveing accepted the
Crowne and Royall Dignity [as][1] aforesaid
Their said Majestyes did become were are
and of right ought to be by the Lawes of
this Realme our Soveraigne Liege Lord and
Lady King and Queene of England France
and Ireland and the Dominions thereunto
belonging in and to whose Princely Persons
the Royall State Crowne and Dignity of
the said Realmes with all Honours Stiles

Titles Regalities Prerogatives Powers Jurisdictions and Authorities to the same belonging and appertaining are most fully rightfully and intirely invested and incorporated united and annexed And for preventing all Questions and Divisions in this Realme by reason of any pretended Titles to the Crowne and for preserveing a Certainty in the Succession thereof in and upon which the Unity Peace Tranquillity and Safety of this Nation doth under God wholly consist and depend The said Lords Spirituall and Temporall and Commons doe beseech their Majestyes That it may be enacted established and declared That the Crowne and Regall Government of the said Kingdoms and Dominions with all and singular the Premisses thereunto belonging and appertaining shall bee and continue to their said Majestyes and the Survivour of them dureing their Lives and the Life of the Survivour of them And that the entire perfect and full Exercise of the Regall Power and Government be onely in and executed by his Majestie in the Names of both their Majestyes dureing their joynt Lives And after their deceases the said Crowne and Premisses shall be and remaine to the Heires of the Body of her Majestie and for default of such Issue to her Royall Highnesse the Princess Anne of Denmarke and the Heires of her Body and for default of such Issue to the Heires of the Body of his said Majestie And thereunto the said Lords Spirituall and Temporall and Commons doe in the Name of all the People aforesaid most humbly and faithfully submitt themselves their Heires and Posterities for ever and doe faithfully promise That they will stand to maintaine and defend their said Majesties and alsoe the

Limitation and Succession of the Crowne herein specified and contained to the utmost of their Powers with their Lives and Estates against all Persons whatsoever that shall attempt any thing to the contrary. And whereas it hath beene found by Experience that it is inconsistent with the Safety and Welfare of this Protestant Kingdome to be governed by a Popish Prince or by any King or Queene marrying a Papist the said Lords Spirituall and Temporall and Commons doe further pray that it may be enacted That all and every person and persons that is are or shall be reconciled to or shall hold Communion with the See or Church of Rome or shall professe the Popish Religion or shall marry a Papist shall be excluded and be for ever uncapeable to inherit possesse or enjoy the Crowne and Government of this Realme and Ireland and the Dominions

thereunto belonging or any part of the same
or to have use or exercise any Regall Power
Authoritie or Jurisdiction within the same
[And in all and every such Case or Cases
the People of these Realmes shall be and
are hereby absolved of their Allegiance]²
And the said Crowne and Government
shall from time to time descend to and be
enjoyed by such person or persons being
Protestants as should have inherited and
enjoyed the same in case the said person or
persons soe reconciled holding Communion
or Professing or Marrying as aforesaid were
naturally dead [And that every King and
Queene of this Realme who at any time
hereafter shall come to and succeede in the
Imperiall Crowne of this Kingdome shall
on the first day of the meeting of the first
Parlyament next after his or her comeing to
the Crowne sitting in his or her Throne in

the House of Peeres in the presence of the Lords and Commons therein assembled or at his or her Coronation before such person or persons who shall administer the Coronation Oath to him or her at the time of his or her takeing the said Oath (which shall first happen) make subscribe and audibly repeate the Declaration mentioned in the Statute made in the thirtyeth yeare of the Raigne of King Charles the Second Entituled An Act for the more effectuall Preserveing the Kings Person and Government by disableing Papists from sitting in either House of Parlyament But if it shall happen that such King or Queene upon his or her Succession to the Crowne of this Realme shall be under the Age of twelve yeares then every such King or Queene shall make subscribe and audibly repeate the said Declaration at his or her Coronation or the first day of the meeting of the first Parlyament as aforesaid which shall first happen after such King or Queene shall have attained the said Age of twelve yeares.][3] All which Their Majestyes are contented and pleased shall be declared enacted and established by authoritie of this present Parliament and shall stand remaine and be the Law of this Realme for ever And the same are by their said Majesties by and with the advice and consent of the Lords Spirituall and Temporall and Commons in Parlyament assembled and by the authoritie of the same declared enacted and established accordingly

II.

Exception.

And bee it further declared and enacted by the Authoritie aforesaid That from and after this present Session of Parlyament noe

Dispensation by Non obstante of or to any Statute or any part thereof shall be allowed but that the same shall be held void and of noe effect Except a Dispensation be allowed of in such Statute [and except in such Cases as shall be specially provided for by one or more Bill or Bills to be passed dureing this present Session of Parliament.][4]

III.

Provided that noe Charter or Grant or Pardon granted before the three and twentyeth Day of October in the yeare of our Lord one thousand six hundred eighty nine shall be any wayes impeached or invalidated by this Act but that the same shall be and remaine of the same force and effect in Law and noe other then as if this Act had never beene made.

NOTES
1. Interlined on the Roll.
2. Annexed to the Original Act in a separate Schedule.
3. Annexed to the Original Act in a separate Schedule.
4. Annexed to the Original Act in a separate Schedule.

Jonathan Sumption, Lord Sumption,
is a former Supreme Court Judge and
an award-winning historian.

First published in 2022 by the Bodleian Library
Broad Street, Oxford OX1 3BG
www.bodleianshop.co.uk

ISBN: 978 1 85124 603 8

Publisher: Samuel Fanous
Managing Editor: Susie Foster
Editor: Janet Phillips
Picture Editor: Leanda Shrimpton
Designed and typeset by Dot Little at the Bodleian Library
in 10 on 13.9 Adobe Caslon Pro
Printed and bound by Livonia Print, Latvia,
on 115 gsm Munken Print Cream paper

British Library Catalogue in Publishing Data
A CIP record of this publication is available from the British Library